Bad Catholic Mothers

A Book of Revelations

Lucia Duff Paul and Katie McCollow

iUniverse, Inc.
New York   Bloomington

Bad Catholic Mothers

A Book of Revelations

iUniverse books may be ordered through booksellers or by contacting:
iUniverse
1663 Liberty Drive
Bloomington, IN 47403
www.iuniverse.com
1-800-Authors (1-800-288-4677)

ISBN: 978-1-4401-0531-9 (pbk)
ISBN: 978-1-4401-0532-6 (ebk)

Printed in the United States of America
iUniverse rev. date: 1/08/2009

To the bad Catholic mothers who helped us with this book-we thank you, and hope you'll be part of our next project: *Humorless Martyrs.*

Foreword

Bad Catholic mothers meet, and don't help others.

When your child starts Catholic school, you have confidence that you'll meet like-minded moms. Maybe you'll find a new friend while volunteering for a food drive, or perhaps while helping to stuff bags of supplies for tiny children in South America. Or maybe not.

When my son, Walter brought home his class picture from second grade, I took one look at it and thought, "Damn you, Walter!"

There was his delightful teacher, all his classmates in their navy uniforms, plaster Jesus up on a large crucifix, and Walter, pulling his eyelids back with his index fingers and shoving his nose up with his pinky fingers. Just great. Now he would be forever the child who ruined the class picture.

But wait. Someone else had ruined the photo too! Oh, joy, there was another boy looking as grotesque, nay, more grotesque than Walter.

Who was this child? I must meet his mother. I was sure we'd have a lot in common. I found out that Finbar McCollow was the other mutant in the photo. Eventually I met his mother, Katie, who I mistook for the babysitter because of her youth. But I quickly forgave her once I found out she was hilarious, and had long been a humorous essayist, just like me!

Bad Catholic Mothers was a project I had been thinking about for some time and Katie was just the person to help bring it to life.

In between watching *Rome* and *Gilmore Girls* while the children were in school, working on our writing projects, and praying the rosary (kidding!), Katie and I began to talk to other women, of all ages, about their "bad" Catholic mom experiences.

So put down your Bible, kick off your sensible shoes, and enjoy.

Please remember that our intention with this book is laughter, joy and making fun of ourselves. So, loosen your girdle and have a wee snifter of brandy if you feel yourself getting worked up about anything in here. It always works for us.

Lucia Duff Paul

When Lucia invited me to be part of this project, I was horribly offended.

" I'm not a bad Catholic mother," I told her, but it came out, "Ahm nottabaa kafflick mudder." I was pretty hammered.

I'm joking of course; I wasn't really offended. A little surprised perhaps, mostly to learn I had children. But I was also thrilled to be asked to lend a hand. In fact, I immediately offered to wash her feet with my hair. She declined, I was grateful.

Meeting Lucia was as serendipitous as a Holy day of obligation falling on a Sunday. Our kids oftentimes inspire us to (*ahem*) speak in tongues. We have the same irreverent sense of humor and strangely, the same "I went to Sodom and Gomorrah and came home with a burning bush" t-shirt. I knew we'd be friends.

So we started collecting stories, and after a while I had this epiphany: turns out, the phrase "Bad Catholic Mother" is redundant. I cannot tell you how relieved I am that when I finally get to Purgatory, at least I'll know some people there.

Be a Doubting Thomas no longer. You're not the first woman to tell her children church is closed the morning after Mommy's karaoke party. Isn't it nice to know you're not alone?

Katie McCollow

Section One

Pray for us now, and pretty much all of the time.

"Mommy what are we doing here?" My impatient preschooler asked me during Mass on Easter Sunday.

"We're here because Jesus rose from the dead," I reminded her.

"Yuck!" she bellowed.

My daughter attended a Catholic elementary school run by nuns. One day, Sister Marie called to say she was so sorry about the loss of my father. Huh?

My Dad was upright and breathing just fine, thanks.

It turns out my daughter, during circle time when they prayed for special family needs, had said, "My Grandpa died this weekend."

When I asked her why she would say such a thing she said, "Because I never have any good ones!"

Jesus is Hot

I'm drawn to other Catholic mothers. I mean that in a clean and wholesome way.

I have found a comforting and disturbing kinship with them. A familiar mix of modesty, hard work, shame and self-deprecation that just screams, "I grew up Catholic!"

These are women who work, stay home, volunteer, play golf, guard the Holy Eucharist, do yoga and go to Mass. Sometimes all in one day. These are women you can count on.

I've never been on a mission to alienate any of them. But occasionally, a gal makes a misstep.

When *the Passion of the Christ* came out, my husband and I went to see it with a few other couples, women I had met at my children's school, Holy Spray Tan.

For those of you who didn't brave a viewing of *The Passion*, it is a three-hour armrest grip-fest punctuated by eye shutting and gross-out facial expressions.

But one element of the *Passion* really stood out for me. And that pure and reverential observation was, "Wow! Jesus is smokin'!"

Jim Caviezel/Jesus was a sweaty, muscular manly specimen. He was completely glorious in every way. Wrap him in burlap. Cover him in ashes. The guy is still gorgeous.

But as I learned in my own bad Catholic mothering moment, these things are best left unsaid.

After our group left the movie, we adjourned to the contemplative and restorative oasis that is a sushi bar.

 I sipped my Saketini, and gently polished my impure thoughts about Jesus. The conversation started innocently.

"That sure gets a guy thinking," said a serious husband, a Notre Dame grad who was kickin' it suburban Saturday night-style in a navy Lacoste shirt.

"The suffering!," offered a naturally lovely blonde who had taken perhaps a two-week break from volunteering at school for the birth of her fourth child.

Opinions were being bandied about. Why not add mine?

"I couldn't believe how gorgeous Jesus was," I blurted out. Silence, possibly throughout the entire restaurant.

"Those eyes! That tan! And what a carpenter! Who knew Jesus had arms like that?" I continued.

I was warming to my subject, and making the critical mistake of taking the nervous half-grins of my tablemates as encouragement. This would be just the time to mention my girlhood crush on Jesus.

I helped myself to another dragon roll, "I would just stare at this picture of Jesus at St. Leo's, " I said. "He was kind of a seventies Jesus. The long hair, blue eyes. Hemp shirt open to mid-chest," I finished and waited for agreeing nods.

Anytime now. Come on. No one else thought Jesus was hot?

I need to mention that my husband bears more than a passing resemblance to a hot Jesus.

So I threw him in too.

"Look at him! I took one look and thought, yeah, he sure looks like him. If I can't have the real thing….."

He gave me a silent marriage stare that clearly stated, "I haven't kept my pimp hand strong."

I went too far. But herein lies the rub of the bad Catholic mom. We are largely a funny and fun-loving lot.

The eye contact among the women at the table was obvious, "If she has lustful thoughts about our Savior, our husbands don't stand a chance!"

I excused myself and went to the ladies room.

One of the other women came in and I was sure I was about to get a feel for what 'ole Jesus had been through in the movie. She had gone to St. Mary's and medical school. A deadly "good Catholic mom" combo.

But wait; where there is life, and a bathroom, there is hope.

"Hey," she began. I looked around wildly as if the small area was crammed full of humanity.

"Me?" I squeaked, reaching for the complimentary Jergens Lotion. Good time to moisturize. Who wants to beat up on someone slippery?

"Just so you know," she began.

Oh here it comes. Psalms to be read, dire warnings of my children being outcasts.

" I haven't thought of it in years. But there was a picture in my middle school of Jesus carrying a lamb. He was looking right at me. I've had weird guilt ever since for thinking Jesus was as cute as Leif Garret," she told me without the furtive glancing and shoulder tics that accompanied my confession.

Halleluiah! One of my own. By the time we'd applied lip-gloss, I learned that she also thought Benedictus XVI is our first metrosexual Pope. We agreed it's the red Prada shoes.

We went out to join our table and I felt light, emboldened. Not nearly as deviant and nasty as I'd felt going in.

I looked around the table, and thanks to the bathroom revelation, I felt we might all have religious-induced secrets. Maybe the men were holding warm and confusing feelings for women in light blue bathrobes. Thanks, Virgin Mary portraits!

Bless our souls, I have a feeling we're going to need it.

In social conversation between my sister, with whom I am very close, and our parish priest, my sister and I began to good-naturedly rib each other about who volunteered at church more often. Remembering that she had just brought food to a funeral luncheon, she gloated, "Ha! I win!" and without thinking I blurted out, "F*#* you!" Our priest, who has eight siblings, didn't even flinch.

I was hosting a get-together at my home, a picnic that included adults and children. A neighbor woman climbed up on our trampoline where my seven-year-old son was jumping. Apparently he'd been eavesdropping on my husband and I because he informed her, "My mom says you're an alcoholic!"

Section 2

"And the little children shall lead them…" straight to Hell.

I am a single mom at a very conservative Catholic school.

One morning, I dropped my son at school quite late because we were scrambling (as usual) at home to eat breakfast, find homework, etc. I told him to tell his teacher he had been at the orthodontist.

Just before noon, I get a call from the school principal who says she needs to see me immediately. I race to her office, where she and my son's teacher deliver a long and stern lecture about lying. They placed a lot of emphasis on parents setting an example by promoting truthfulness.

When his teacher questioned the orthodontist visit, my son cracked like an egg, "My Mom told me to say that."

I was in a particularly foul mood and my children were being particularly non-cooperative, especially in the area of finding and putting on their shoes. Finally I got everyone in the car and off to school, and my daughter said to me,

"Mom, Dad's going to be pretty mad at you when he finds out you said the "F" word about a billion times."

Tough Act to Follow

My full name is Mary Katherine; my own mom named me after the mother of all Catholic mothers, the Virgin Mary. But that and the name seems to be where the similarities between us end.

For crying out loud, the cards are stacked against us Catholic gals from the start. To even get into the "mom" club, we have to forfeit the very thing that made Mary's motherhood so remarkable. I have three kids myself. Immaculate Conception…sure…or the results of the movie Ghost, Def Leppard's opus "Pour Some Sugar on Me" and multiple shots of tequila. Tomato, tomahto.

Not only that, but Mary was perfectly willing to boss the very Son of God around. Remember the "water into wine" thing when Jesus griped at her "Woman, what has that to do with me? My time has not yet come."

Wouldn't you love to believe that Mary's response was to pull him aside and hiss "Just do it, you little *snot*. People are leaving and they haven't even cut the cake. And who are you calling *'woman'?*" with a little smack upside his head.

I'm sure she was nicer about it, but she got what she wanted, right? The closest I've ever come to eliciting a culinary miracle of that magnitude was forcing my husband to find me some tacos at three a.m. when I was eight months pregnant. That was also around the same time I started begging for the epidural. Deliver a baby in a stable; are you kidding me?

When my first child was born and the doctor tried to lay the baby on my chest, I took one whiff of my sticky bundle of joy and asked the nurse if she wouldn't mind "washing it off first". I don't care how friendly the beasts in the barn were; if I'd been told to go sleep with them when I was in labor, you can bet your last donkey there would've been dead innkeeper all over that silent night.

Mary wouldn't have been too busy pilfering Kit Kats out of her child's Halloween bag to remember the All Saint's Day mass. I sent my daughter into the "Parade of Saints" wearing a terry-cloth swimsuit cover-up and the cape from her brother's batman costume on her head.

Mary wouldn't have hated Christmas concerts, either. No way would she have considered tromping out into a cold December night to watch other people's children butcher "Good King Wenceslaus" a rotten way to spend an evening.

She would've volunteered at Jesus' school with a loving smile in her heart, like a good mom is supposed to. When told by Jesus' teacher that he couldn't do fractions, surely she wouldn't have replied, "You know what he can do? He can be your problem until three o'clock.".

I doubt she would've joked that the "The Da Vinci Code" was a heresy on the grounds that Jesus wasn't married to Mary Magdalene, they were just friends with benefits. She might've chuckled at the thought in private, I mean c'mon, she was human, but she would never have said it out loud in front of her mother's entire book club.

There is something deeply deficient in me.

It's not all bad though; there are times when I feel I've lived up to my namesake.

Not long ago, I was in my kitchen and my kids were roughhousing in the next room. They were laughing and shrieking and suddenly I heard my eight-year-old son holler gleefully at his older sister,

"Ahhh haaaa! You hit me right in the balls!"

The record scratched to a stop, birds hung motionless in the sky, the geezer in the corner cocked his proverbial shotgun. I walked slowly into the room where they were, looked at the boy and said sternly,

"Your body is a beautiful gift from God, and to refer to it in such a crude way is an insult to Him. Those are not your *balls*."

"I'm sorry mom," he stammered.

"Those are your *nuts,"* I replied, and walked back into the kitchen.

Surely Mary appreciates a well-timed punch line, right?

"Bad Catholic Mom". I guess, if you feel the need to fling a few stones at me from that there glass house. But I take comfort in the fact that even the worst Catholic mom is still a pretty decent Episcopalian.

I took my kids to see the uber-violent movie musical, "Sweeney Todd," on Christmas Eve.

My young daughter was having a difficult time with another girl at school. I told her that if the other girl was being mean to her, the best course of action was to steer clear of her until things blew over. The next day, the other little girl's mother called me, concerned.

My daughter had given her daughter a note that read, "I can't play with you because I think you are mean and so does my mom."

Section 3

Bad Catholic Moms Through the Ages

My grandmother was diagnosed with liver cancer at the age of eighty-three. In her lifetime, she had already survived abandonment by a scoundrel, raised five children, run a successful business, and lived long enough to enjoy the company of seventeen grandchildren, and four great-grandchildren.

So when the medical experts at the hospital presented her treatment options, she declined them all and came up with her own: "I want to go to my daughter's house, drink a lot, and take pleasure in my family."

And that's exactly what she did for the six weeks until she died.

My mother told a potential landlord that she had only three children (his limit) when she actually had five. He rented us the apartment, and every time he visited the property, she sent two of us away until he left.

Don't Give Me That Beatitude.

I was twelve years old that summer morning and crestfallen at my mother's instructions: we were going to confession at the cathedral. Confession began at three o'clock; by which time I was to have my conscience examined and be cleaned up and dressed properly.

I hated this.

I did not want to examine my conscience. I was twelve years old, after all, and was worried about what I might find in there—I had as much a life as any of my friends, and was appalled at the very idea of confiding to some priest the deeds, words and thoughts that I had deeded, worded and thought. I had visions of the confessor as I whispered my sins shouting in disbelief, rushing out of his stall into mine and grabbing me, dragging me out into the church and shouting to all the other penitents, including my mother, *"Do you know what he did? Do you know what thoughts he took pleasure in? DO YOU?"*

And then he would tell them! And what would happen to me? What would be done with me? A life of shame and rejection was only hours away.

How was I going to get out of this?

In mid-afternoon we headed down to the cathedral.

"Why do we have to go to the cathedral?" I whined, thinking that following my exposure as a shameful wretch

I could more easily escape and get lost forever in the countryside around our own parish church.

"Because," my mother explained, "It's handy to some stores and I want to do some shopping afterward."

"You mean after confession?"

"Yes. After confession." She looked at me as though I had said something odd. Little did she realize that the end of life as we knew it was rapidly approaching. Oh, how she would curse the day this rotten apple of a son had been born to her!

When we reached the cathedral, things got worse. She marched right up to the shortest line, to the confessional manned by the cathedral's pastor, whom I will refer to as Father BigNoise. He was so famous for his nasty temper that the local newspaper once published a feature story about him, told how one Sunday he had locked all the doors of the cathedral after everyone was inside so that no one could leave early. Then he delivered a forty-five minute sermon about how disrespectful, swinish worshippers who left early in order to go outside and smoke cigarettes on the front steps and leave their filthy, discarded butts on the ground were headed to a bad place.

When the fire marshal got wind of how Father BigNoise had imprisoned his congregation, he delivered him a stern lecture of his own, assuring him that if he ever again locked up the cathedral when if was full of people he would quickly find himself headed to a bad place.

Father BigNoise refrained hereafter from locking in his worshippers, but he never failed to pack his lengthy sermons chock full of slanders about the fire marshal.

Now, here were my mother and I, standing in line outside the infamous man's confessional, listening to him hiss and rumble at some poor soul. And the poor soul, a really old man of maybe forty years, comes out looking downcast and chastened, and I am thinking how lucky he is, how I wish that I were in his place.

Now I hear Father BigNoise growling and snarling at my mother, my sainted mother who never in her life has committed a sin. He is dressing her down.

My mother's parents had emigrated from Ireland, and she had grown up in a large and spirited family whose members had been taught to stand up for themselves. When my mom got angry she tended to talk in an Irish brogue.

"Aarra, shat app!" I hear her say to Father BigNoise. *"Who d'ya think yar talkin' to?"*

His disrespectful manner had angered her.

And out of the confessional she marches, and looks at me, with my eyebrows up nearly to my hairline, and she smiles.

And I smile at my tough, bad, Irish Catholic mom. I am filled with pride in her, and I know that everything is going to be all right.

My mother forgot all about my first communion. She put me in a bright red dress and dropped me off at the church that Sunday morning, alone.

One night when I was about eleven, I slept over at my beloved Grandmother's house on a school night. The next morning, she made me a ham sandwich to take to school for lunch.

"But Nana, wait! It's Friday, I can't eat meat," I reminded her in a panic.

"Oh, poo," she said. "Eat the sandwich. God doesn't want to see good ham go to waste."

My grandmother's portrait hangs in my living room. In it she strikes a regal pose, her hair piled high, chin jutting out proudly, brown eyes snapping. She looks like a defiant woman capable of stirring controversy, and she was. In fact, she hadn't been showing up for the sittings with the painter, but meeting her secret lover instead, a fact that came to light when her husband unveiled the portrait and exclaimed, "But Eleanor, your eyes are blue."

Section Four

Oh Unholy Night

One Christmas night, I had just about had it. I was exhausted from the weeks of preparation and the excitement of the day. My children were arguing over a bag of marshmallows. I grabbed the bag away and told them to knock it off. They started wailing again, so I threw the marshmallows at them and said, "Eat them. Eat them until you die."

One Christmas morning, I was racing to get everyone in the car, loading the presents and food I was bringing to my Mom's. None of my children, or husband was helping, hurrying or listening. I stood in the driveway and yelled, "It's f% *^\$*# Christmas, and we need to hurry. Now get in the car!" Just then our neighbors (calm and serene) walked by.

"Merry Christmas!" I called and waved. Fooling no one.

Each year, we let one of our three children design our Christmas card. We tell then to draw something that signifies Christmas to them. Last year, for her turn as illustrator, our youngest daughter presented us with a crayon drawing of the devil with a pig nose. We decided not to send a card last year.

It's all Eve's fault, I don't even like apples.

I've been hijacked. A pirate has come aboard me who, thus far, has remained faceless and nameless, but demands are being made loud and clear.

"Eat something! No, not a salad... A donut! Now go throw it up!"

"Go pee. Again! Again!"

"Yell at your husband for no reason! Now cry!"

"Go to sleep! HAHA!! Good luck with that one, sucka!"

That's right, I'm a bad-Catholic-mom-to-be, in trouble. Let me clarify: I'm not "in trouble" like a bobby-soxer on her way to visit Grandma for nine months; I am both of age and married. I'm "in trouble" with my mom because I got married in Las Vegas, and not by a priest.

"I'm looking out for your baby's soul!" she said to me.

Now before you go assuming that my mom and dad are the overbearing types who force their will on their children, let me tell you that they are not. I could tell my mom felt uncomfortable even suggesting to me how to run my own life, and therefore realized just how strongly she felt about the matter. My parents are absolutely wonderful people. They love my husband dearly, even though he is not Catholic and he is divorced. (If either of those things ever did bother them, they had the class not to let it show.)

So anyway, I called my priest- the one who baptized and confirmed me- to ask about getting my marriage blessed by the church. I tried; then I took a nap. What else can I do?

I have to admit I've never been more excited in my life (Excited like when that kid from The Ring crawled out of the TV. But this one isn't coming out my TV). And I'm not even allowed to calm my nerves in my usual fashion of downing vodka tonics while soaking in a Jacuzzi. To be fair, while the baby taketh away- cocktails, cute jeans, rational thought-the baby also giveth: body acne, a squishy backside, and the best true excuse I have ever had for getting out of anything I don't feel like doing. Like, oh, attending mass. Under normal circumstances I am a regular at one mass or another around town, but I think God understands that by the time I get up, shower, get dressed, and drive to church another nap is about hit me like a Peterbilt. That I'm pregnant during Lent does not help. I've been a church fainter since I was nine years old, and incense doesn't exactly help wake me up. Or keep my breakfast down.

Also, I did not give up anything for Lent. I grew up believing that travelers, the sick and/or elderly, and preggos are exempt. And at our house Sundays were a day off for eveybody; if you gave up chocolate for Lent, then on Sunday you chugged chocolate chips from the second you got home from church 'til the minute you went to bed that night.

So, no mass and no giving up anything for Lent. But I've given up a lot anyway, and for much longer than forty days. I've also been listening to my Jesus Christ

Superstar soundtrack everyday, so don't judge me, Mr. Stonethrower.

Is all the sacrifice worth it? How should I know, I don't even know this kid yet! But will it make me a better Catholic? Probably... I mean, I have to go to church for the baptism, right?

The day after Thanksgiving, I brought my children downtown to see the Christmas display on the eighth floor of Marshall Fields. The wait to get in was over an hour, so I took them across the street to a bar and they spent the evening watching mom drink Irish car bombs instead.

My six-year old son gave me a homemade Mother's Day card. On the front he had drawn a picture of me standing in front of a row of barbells. I was pleased that he associated me with an obvious symbol of good health.

"Are those barbells next to me," I asked him, smug in the knowledge that I was Setting a Good Example.

"No Mom! They're wine glasses!"

Section 5

Weapons of Mass Destruction

There is always a lot of speculation by children about what nuns wear under their habits. My five-year-old son took it to a new level when he yelled, "I just know that's a man under there!" in front of a nun on his first day of kindergarten.

I took my eight-year old daughter to Mass one Sunday. "Why are we here," she moaned. "To give thanks to God," I said. "Can't we just send him a thank you note?" she replied.

The not-so-virgin mother.

I stumbled into motherhood. That's a fact. My very own, teenaged pregnancy. Two months shy of my twentieth birthday, I gave birth to a ten- pound baby boy. Unwed.

That sounds so awful, right? "An Unwed Mother." An instant identity. I was Party Girl before, so I guess this was the next logical step. My sister gave me a rosary as some kind of what, recognition? Congratulations? Instruction? Deterrent? It was lost on me. I said thank you and wished it would transform into a roll of quarters so I could do laundry.

I spent the next four years in that "unwed" state. I wore lots of rings in an attempt to confuse the public. "Is she married? So many rings... who could know?" Not believing myself to be Catholic anymore ("what do they know, anyway?") I wished things to be different in my life. Wishing seemed much more grown up than praying. I wished that I could have a "normal" life. I daydreamed on the city bus. Me, my Baby Boy, and a man with fuzzy features. Tall, though. Tall and funny. I married the Tall, Funny Man. No church wedding for us. No, sir! No Church was going to tell us about our love. We were on our own. Just the three, make that four, of us.

My "normal" life had arrived. Two baby boys plus one tall, funny man. I felt good. Diapers, coloring books, tinker-toys. This wasn't so hard! I didn't know how to cook or actually do much of anything in the "domestic sciences." Being a middle child of eight, you'd think I would have learned to keep a house in ship-shape. In fact, I only knew one eighth of everything. I could peel the potatoes, but had no idea how they got from that state to a steamy mushy pile on my plate. I could fill water glasses very efficiently. Unfortunately, peeled potatoes and glasses of ice-water don't a dinner make. When it was just me and Baby Boy, I could just order a hoagie and make a picnic on the living room floor. Normal was hard.

I stumbled into motherhood and marriage without a clue. I had no idea what I was getting myself into. Why would someone do something like that?

"Hey, look at that pitch-black and seemingly endless pit! I'd like to jump in there!"

What allows human beings to take those crazy, life-changing, pit-jumping risks? It can't be stupidity because even a stupid person has enough sense to not jump into the pitch-black pit. This thought just happened to cross my mind while I was peeling potatoes with my five-year-old (who is now sixteen). He had recently seen a cartoon depicting cats with harps and little wings floating up to the pearly gates.

He was curious. He wanted to know more. So many questions. I was ashamed! What kind of unwed-turned-wed mother had I turned out to be?! What a crummy mother. I promised myself (but not God, that would be, like, crazy) that I would be better. It would start tonight, at the dinner table.

"Thank you Lord, for these yummy potatoes and perfectly chilled water."

My teenaged daughter had a baby out of wedlock. I told her younger sisters she had adopted him.

I didn't baptize my daughter until she was eight. I made up a baptismal date on her application to the Catholic grade school we wanted her to attend.

My three-year-old daughter was rooting through my purse during mass one Sunday and found something I'd left in there from an evening out with my girlfriends the night before.

She held up her find and asked me loudly, "Mom, do you want a cigarette?"

My son didn't receive his first communion until he was thir-teen.

At Saturday afternoon reconciliation, I instructed my kids to wait for me in the otherwise empty church while I confessed.

In the confessional I asked the priest for forgiveness for losing patience with my *ahem* high-energy children and as he absolved me and gave me a pep talk, the two of us could hear a noisy fist-fight break out between my kids outside.

"Dammit," I muttered.

The priest started to laugh.

At my kids' Catholic school, they routinely are asked to go around the room and say how often they go to Mass. I tell my kids to say we go to Mass regularly when we don't. They go during the school week; I figure they're covered.

Section 6

Bad Catholic Wives

My mother baptized my non-Catholic husband while he was sleeping during a football game. I didn't believe that it was really "binding." A few years later I casually asked a priest, "Say Father O'Connor, if someone, no one I know personally of course, but if a non-priest baptizes someone, is it really a baptism?" Turns out it is. My mother is free to save mortal souls at will. This is not good news.

My parents loaned my son an ebony rosary that Mother Teresa gave my grandmother. My son lost it his First Communion year. I bought a pretty good replica and rubbed salt on it and banged on it with a hammer to "age" it before giving it back.

My father was out of town on a business trip, and my mom often complained that she didn't sleep well when he wasn't home. But this particular morning, my mother had an unusual air of serenity and calm.

"Children, the Blessed Virgin visited me last night."

We kept eating our Count Chocula and looked at each other suspiciously.

"What'd she say?" my brother asked.

"Nothing. She stood at the end of the bed in silence. But I know she has chosen me for a reason."

My Dad returned that night, and heard the story. He went upstairs to change and came back downstairs a short time later.

"Maura, I think I can explain the appearance of the Blessed Virgin-you left the ironing board standing on end next to the bureau."

So much for holy visitations.

When I arrived in this country during World War II, I spoke only French, and was trying very hard to learn English. While waiting for my husband to return home, I went to live with my mother-in-law in northern Minnesota. We went to confession, and I told the priest (as best I could), that if he could just say the sin, I would tell him yes or no, and how many times I had committed the sin.

He obliged. Adultery? Yes, seven or eight times. Theft? Gosh, yes, several times a week. Don't ask me what I thought he was saying because I couldn't tell you. I was confessing left and right to everything under the sun. At some point, he left the confessional, went out to my mother-in-law and said, "I can't help you. You need to find a French church."

I gave my children snacks to eat while I went to confession. Rule followers to the core, they asked if it was OK to eat in church. An older lady came up and chastised them I'm sure she was delighted to hear, "It's none of your damn business" as a response!

Adjust Your Beatitude

1. Blessed is the school bus; for it takes the children away.

2. Blessed is the back pew; it allows for an early exit.

3. Blessed are the tinted windows; I can stay in my pajamas when I drop the children off..

4. Blessed are they that hunger and thirst for justice; and for brownies and red wine.

5. Blessed are they who mourn; but have faith, for a new season of the Bachelor will be on again soon.

6. Blessed are the clean of house and coordinated of outfit; I'll try not to hold it against them.

7. Blessed are the peacemakers, and the hair color makers, the trashy novel makers, and whoever invented footbaths.

8. Blessed are they who suffer persecution for not volunteering to be room mom or playground attendant.